QUAKES, FLOODS AND OTHER DISASTERS

Fred Martin

Quakes, Floods and Other Disasters

Rigby is a part of Harcourt Education
a division of Reed International Books Australia Pty Ltd
20 Thackray Road, Port Melbourne, Victoria 3207
rigby.com.au
info@hi.com.au

Offices in Sydney, Brisbane, Perth and Adelaide. Associated
companies, branches and representatives throughout the world.

Text by Fred Martin
Designed by M2
Illustrations by Hardlines, M2 and Lewis Chandler (p. 18)

Film supplied by TypeScan, Australia
Printed in China by Midas Printing (Asia) Ltd.

National Library of Australia
ISBN 978 0 7312 3282 6
ISBN 0 7312 3282 8

Acknowledgments for photographs: A & M Breuil /Still Pictures, p. 21; Richard
Ashworth/ Robert Harding Picture Library, p. 20; Archive, p. 4; Lynette Cook/ Science
Photo Library, p. 12; Mark Edwards/Still Pictures, pp. 10, 22; R. Holcomb, p. 15; Keith
Kent/Science Photo Library, p. 5; The National History Museum, title page and page
26; Anna Piantanida/ Still Pictures, p. 25; Popperfoto/Reuters, p. 7; Reuters, p. 18; ©
Galen Rowell/ CORBIS (APL); p. 18; Rev. Ronald Royer/ Science Photo Library, p. 27;
Sean Sprague, p. 16; Werner Stoy/ Bruce Coleman Ltd, p. 14;

Contents

LOOKING FOR ANSWERS

What is a natural disaster?

Earthquakes, floods, hurricanes and volcanic eruptions can all cause deaths, injuries and enormous damage. Events such as these are called natural disasters. Some natural disasters only last for a few seconds or a few hours, though the problems they cause can last for years. An earthquake, for example, can last for seconds but destroy a whole city. Other disasters take several months to happen, such as when there is too little rain and crops do not grow.

Earthquakes destroy people's homes.

Lightning, which can start fires, is caused when an electrical spark jumps between the clouds and the ground.

Questions about natural disasters

People need to find out more about natural disasters. Some questions are easy to answer, such as where a disaster has happened and what damage has been done. It is not as easy to explain what causes a natural disaster or to predict when the next one will happen.

In the past, natural disasters were blamed on "the gods". Now scientists know more about the natural forces that cause them. Although these events can be a disaster for people, they are all simply part of how nature works.

Nature, however, still has many secrets. This is why it is still so hard to predict the next natural disaster, and what will happen when it begins.

RIVER FLOODS

Fighting floods in China

During the summer of 1998, people in China fought to stop their rivers from flooding. A flood is when water from a river flows over the land. The river Yangtze was one of the biggest rivers that flooded. Farmers and soldiers tried to make the river banks stronger and higher with stones and sandbags.

They were successful in some places. In others, the rivers either burst through their banks or flowed over the top. Once this happened, there was nothing to stop the water from spreading across the flat valley bottoms where people had their homes and farms.

What caused the disaster?

The main reason for the floods was that there was more rain than usual. At first, most of the rain sank into the ground. After more rain, the ground became so wet that no more rain could sink into it. It continued to rain. Next, the rainwater began to flow quickly off the ground and into the rivers. Before long, the rivers were so full that they began to overflow and flood.

Sometimes there is more than one reason for a flood. If mountain snow and ice melt in spring, at the same time as there is heavy rain, streams can quickly become raging torrents. The extra water then flows down to the lowland rivers. When this happens, people need to watch out for floods.

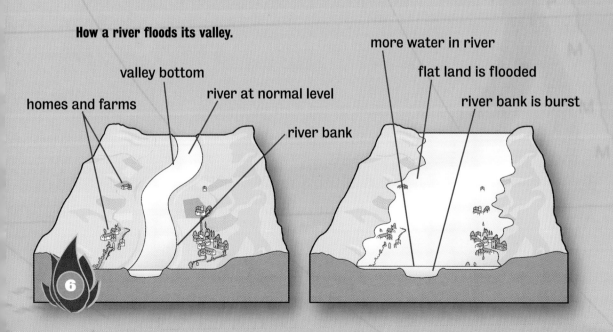

How a river floods its valley.

homes and farms

valley bottom

river at normal level

river bank

more water in river

flat land is flooded

river bank is burst

People made homeless by the floods in China.

THE 1998 RIVER FLOODS IN CHINA

- About 2600 people were killed during the floods.

- At least twenty million homes were washed away.

- One city was saved from flooding by blowing up the banks with dynamite and flooding farmland instead.

- The last bad floods in China were in 1954, when 30 000 people died.

THE STRONGEST WINDS

Measuring the wind

The wind is one of nature's most common and destructive forces. Although it is nothing more than moving air, the wind can cause enormous damage.

Wind speed is measured on the Beaufort Scale. The strongest winds on this scale blow at force 12, called hurricane force.

The fastest and most violent winds of all are in a tornado. A tornado is a very narrow funnel of air that spirals up from the ground to the sky. The wind speed can be up to 800 km per hour, which is too fast to be measured on the Beaufort Scale.

The Beaufort Scale

0 calm smoke rises straight up		**6** strong breeze hard to use an umbrella	
1 light air smoke starts to drift		**7** moderate gale hard to walk into the wind	
2 light breeze leaves rustle		**8** fresh gale twigs break off trees	
3 gentle breeze flags wave		**9** strong gale roof tiles move	
4 moderate breeze small branches move		**10** storm trees uprooted	
5 fresh breeze small trees sway		**11** violent storm houses damaged	
		12 hurricane destruction of many buildings	

Air and clouds spiral out at the top.

Air continues to spiral upwards to form dense clouds.

Air rotates around the centre.

Hot, moist air spirals quickly upwards towards cold, dry air.

More air is sucked into the low pressure area at the bottom.

What makes the wind blow?

Air is made up of many tiny particles called molecules. When the air is cold, the molecules are very close together. When the air is warm, the molecules spread out. Warm air with fewer molecules is lighter than cold air that has more molecules. The scientific name for these different weights of air is air pressure. An area of high pressure is when the air is sinking. An area of low pressure is caused by rising air. Wind occurs when warm air rises and an area of low pressure develops beneath it. Air moves in from an area of high pressure to replace the rising air.

Why does a tornado cause so much damage?

The pressure in the centre of a tornado is very low. As a tornado passes a building, the air pressure outside the building suddenly becomes much lower than the pressure inside. The building is not strong enough to hold the pressure in, so windows are blown out and, in extreme cases, the whole building explodes. The safest place to be during a tornado is in a cellar under the house.

FACTS ABOUT HURRICANES AND TORNADOES

- A hurricane is also called a typhoon or cyclone.
- In the USA, a tornado is also called a twister.
- Tornadoes in the USA are mostly in the central plains, also called "tornado alley".

WHERE THE EARTH SHAKES

Why do earthquakes only happen in some places?

Why is it that news reports about earthquakes always seem to be from the same places? The same regions seem to suffer from earthquakes over and over again.

The strongest earthquakes are in places where there are giant cracks called fault lines through the Earth's surface. These fault lines divide the Earth's outer layer, called the crust, into giant slabs called plates. Forces inside the Earth push and pull the plates, making them move. A sudden jerk along a fault line causes an earthquake.

45°

Houses destroyed by an earthquake in Turkey.

Earthquake damage

A strong earthquake in some countries can cause enormous damage and kill thousands of people in seconds. In 1993, about 20 000 people died in one short earthquake in India. On 17 August 1999, an earthquake in Turkey, measuring 7.4 on the Richter Scale, killed over 17 000 people. There are also strong earthquakes in the USA, but they do not kill as many people because many of the buildings are strong enough to survive an earthquake.

There are some earthquakes in Australia, such as the earthquake that hit Newscastle, New South Wales in 1989, but they are generally not very strong. This is because, as shown on the map below, Australia is not near any of the major fault lines.

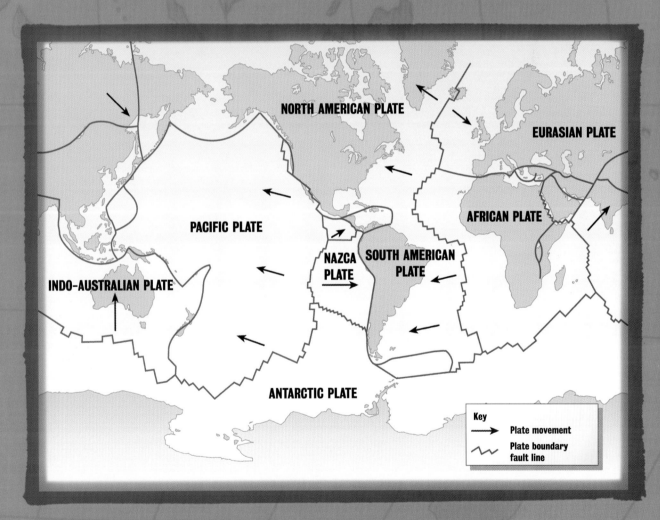

The Earth's plates and major fault lines.

DISASTER ON THE COAST

Giant waves

A tidal wave can be bigger than a two-storey house. A tidal wave is also called a tsunami (pronounced *sue-naa-me*), from two Japanese words, "tsu" meaning a harbour and 'nami' meaning a wave.

A tsunami crashing on to the shore.

What causes a tsunami?

A tsunami can be caused by an earthquake that shakes the sea bed, sometimes hundreds of kilometres out to sea. An erupting volcano can have the same effect. The sea bed heaves, and so does the water above it. This starts a long, low wave that ripples out at great speed towards the coast. The wave can travel at several hundred kilometres per hour. As the tsunami approaches the shore, it moves over shallower water and begins to build up. It gradually becomes a roaring wall of water that crashes on to the shore.

The New Guinea disaster

A tsunami struck the north coast of Papua New Guinea in August 1998. The people had no time to get away. Homes were smashed, farmland was ruined and at least 2000 people were killed.

In time, the survivors will move back and rebuild their homes, although there is no reason why another tidal wave could not strike again. People who live near the sea in areas where there are earthquakes always live with the risk of a tsunami.

A tsunami spreads out from the centre of an underwater earthquake.

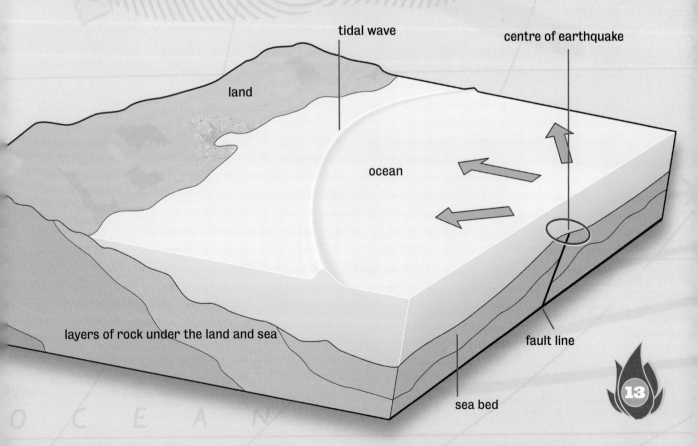

VOLCANO WATCHING

A spectacular event

An erupting volcano is one of nature's most spectacular events. There is no way to stop it from happening. All that scientists can do to help people escape from danger is to try to predict when a volcano will erupt.

How can a volcano eruption be predicted?

Sometimes, a volcano gives clues that it is going to erupt. In the weeks and days before it erupts, hot molten rock called magma moves up into the volcano from deep inside the Earth. This makes the volcano swell. Instruments placed on the slopes are able to measure the change. Another clue is that gases sometimes start to rise from the volcano. There may also be some small eruptions and local earthquakes before a big eruption.

Lava flowing down the slopes of an erupting volcano.

Hard to predict

One problem with trying to predict an eruption is that these clues are not always evident. A second problem is that many volcanoes are in remote places where there are no scientists and no instruments, therefore the clues go unnoticed.

Scientists can study a volcano's history to try to predict what might happen when it erupts. Some erupt like an explosion, sending lumps of rock and ash high into the air. Others erupt more gently, sending rivers of molten lava down their slopes.

There is a lot more that scientists need to find out about volcanoes before they can predict exactly when and how a volcano will erupt.

A scientist studying lava flowing under a cooled lava crust.

LIVING WITH DANGER

Why do people live in places where natural disasters may occur?

It is sometimes hard to understand why people live in places where there may be a natural disaster. It may just be that people find it hard to move away from their homes, but sometimes there are other reasons why people choose to live near the site of a natural disaster.

Farmers growing crops near a volcano in the Philippines.

Living near a volcano

There are some good reasons why people live near volcanoes. In Iceland, the hot rock near volcanoes heats water in the ground, and people use this hot water to heat their homes. Near some volcanoes in New Zealand, the climate acts on the volcanic deposits to produce steam, which is used to generate electricity. In Indonesia and Japan, heavy rain and strong sunlight break down lava until it becomes soil that is very good for growing crops. A volcano can also attract tourists, such as those who go to see Vesuvius in Italy.

Types of volcano

To live near a volcano, it is useful to know how often it is likely to erupt. There are three types of volcano:

 active volcanoes still regularly erupt;

 dormant volcanoes have not erupted for several hundred years, but may still erupt;

 extinct volcanoes will never erupt again.

People live on or near all three types, though extinct volcanoes are the only ones that are really safe.

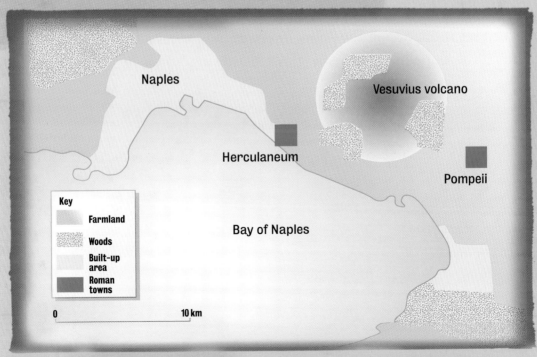

Naples

Vesuvius volcano

Herculaneum

Pompeii

Key

Farmland

Woods

Built-up area

Roman towns

Bay of Naples

0   10 km

The Italian city of Naples has spread close to Vesuvius, the volcano that destroyed the Roman towns of Pompeii and Herculaneum. Vesuvius is still an active volcano.

DISASTER ON THE MOUNTAINS

Avalanches

Every year, millions of people go skiing and every year, people are killed by avalanches. Avalanches tend to occur in Europe and North and South America. Avalanches are usually caused by a rise in temperature, a storm or human activity such as the weight of people on a vulnerable spot. Avalanches can occur very quickly and with very little warning. There is very little chance of surviving an avalanche because of both the impact and the freezing temperatures.

How do avalanches occur?

There are two types of avalanches—the powder-snow avalanche and the slab avalanche. The powder-snow type can be very dangerous as it begins from a single point and expands as it gains speed descending down the mountain. In fact, the route of this type of avalanche resembles an upside-down "v".

The slab avalanche is a thick layer of snow and ice that has not properly joined the layer below it. Consequently, the top layer is supporting its own weight on a slope and any trigger, such as a storm, a change in the temperature or human activity can set it off. When the snow layer can no longer support its weight, it slides down the slope like a pane of glass, shattering under its own weight.

Powder avalanche

Slab avalanche

An avalanche in Europe

On 23 February 1999, an avalanche buried the tiny town of Galtuer in the Austrian Alps. Throughout the night, the town was blocked off from all help because of raging snowstorms. The next afternoon, another avalanche hit the village of Valzur, three kilometres away and thirty-eight people were killed.

Surveying the wreckage after the devastating avalanche that hit the village of Galtuer.

Preventing avalanches

There are several things that can be done to prevent avalanches or to reduce their impact. Fences can be built to prevent great slabs of snow and ice falling. Roofs of buildings can be sloped so that the snow slides off and, in some countries, small explosives are set off to stop huge amounts of snow and ice collecting. Forests and trees also provide a very natural protection from avalanches.

UP IN FLAMES

Fire in the bushlands

Fire burns both plants and animals. One way that a fire can start naturally is when a white hot streak of lightning hits the ground.

The central bushland areas of Australia and Africa have a dry season when there is often no rain for up to six months. During this season, rivers dry up and the grass becomes extremely dry. If lightning hits the ground, a fire can easily start, and the slightest wind will fan the fire, quickly spreading it across large areas. Some animals survive by running away or by hiding underground, but others are not so lucky. Sometimes people are trapped in bushland fires, and lives and homes are lost.

A bush fire.

Can a natural disaster do any good?

After the fire has died out, burnt ash from dead plants is left on the ground. When it rains again, the ash is washed into the soil, making the soil fertile so that more plants can grow. Seeds already in the ground grow quickly because the fire has cleared away the old plants. There are some plants whose seeds only begin to germinate after they have been exposed to the intense heat of a fire.

Before long, the bushland grows again with fresh young plants. The animals start to return, and eventually the landscape looks like it did before. Fire is one of nature's ways of helping new plants to grow and maintaining the bushland.

New plants grow quickly after a fire.

DROUGHT AND FAMINE

Rains that fail

A famine is a time when food is scarce, so people do not have enough to eat. A principal cause of famine is drought. During a drought, rainfall is unusually low so crops fail to grow.

In some parts of Africa, such as Sudan, Mali and Ethiopia, the amount of rain can vary from year to year. When the rain fails, there is a drought. As a result, crops do not grow, animals die of thirst and people go hungry.

Watering plants in a dry part of Africa.

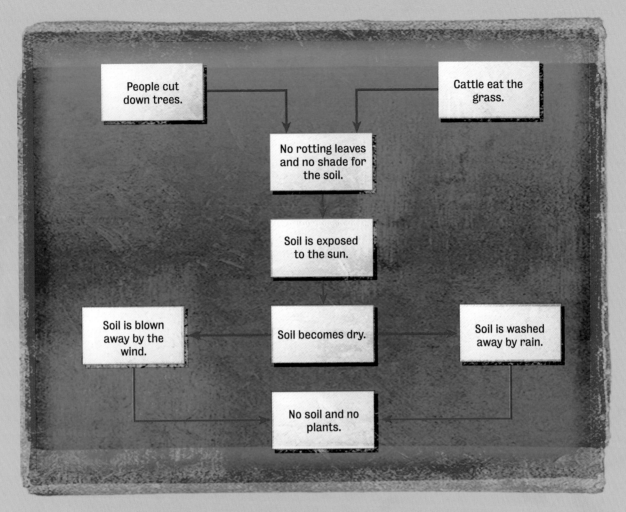

How people and their animals make a drought worse.

Can people make a natural disaster worse?

The effects of a drought can be made worse by people. This happens when people cut down trees for firewood and to get more land for farming. Without shade from the sun, and with no more rotting leaves to enrich it, the soil turns to dust that is useless for growing crops. Without trees to protect it, the soil is exposed, so it is easily washed away by heavy rain or blown away by the wind. Another problem is caused by over-grazing, when too many cattle or sheep eat the grass, making the soil dry and useless.

Wars can make a famine even worse. In recent years there have been wars in places where drought already makes it hard for people to survive.

TRAPPED IN THE "GREENHOUSE"

Global warming

In recent years, the world has had some of the hottest summers ever recorded. Scientists believe that this is proof that the Earth is getting warmer, and have called this "global warming". Further evidence of global warming may be a giant sheet of ice that broke away from the Arctic Sea ice pack and floated south into the Atlantic Ocean.

What causes global warming?

It is thought that global warming is caused by the gases that people are putting into the air by burning coal, petrol and trees. These gases are known as "greenhouse gases". This is because they let in the sun's heat, but instead of it escaping back to space again, the gases trap the heat and keep it in the Earth's atmosphere.

Icebergs break away from an ice shelf as the air becomes warmer.

What effects will global warming have in the future?

If global warming continues, there could be many more natural disasters because of changes in the weather. In some places, there could be longer droughts. In others, the extra heat could start more hurricanes and tornadoes. There could be more rain, so there would be more flooding. As the oceans become warmer, the water will expand and cause the sea level to rise, leading to problems of flooding around the coast.

If all this happens, it will be because people have not considered how their actions affect the ecological balance of the planet.

THE WORLD'S BIGGEST DISASTER

About sixty-five million years ago, dinosaurs were the biggest and most powerful animals on Earth. Then suddenly there was an enormous explosion as the Earth was hit by something from space. Millions of tons of rock, dust and gases were blasted high into the atmosphere. A tidal wave spread out, drowning everything in its path. Fires broke out, burning vast areas of trees and other plants. Millions of animals were instantly killed by the blast.

For the next six months, dust from the explosion blocked out the sun. Plants died and there was nothing for the plant-eating dinosaurs to eat. The Earth also became too cold for the dinosaurs. Only the small animals that lived under the ground were able to survive.

Dinosaurs were the most powerful animals on Earth.

A comet hurtling through space.

Why did this disaster happen?

Scientists have found evidence that a comet or a meteor from space collided with the Earth, causing widespread devastation. They have found the remains of a crater where the Earth was hit on the Yucatan peninsula in Mexico. They have also found a thin layer of dust just above the rocks containing the last fossils of dinosaurs. It is thought that this layer is the dust that settled back to the ground after the explosion.

It looks as if the puzzle of why the dinosaurs became extinct may have been answered at last.

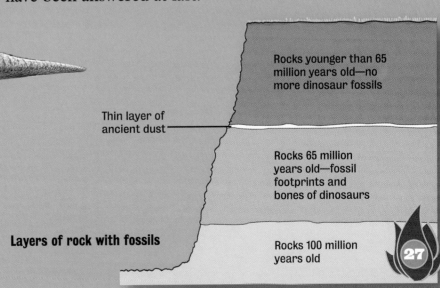

Layers of rock with fossils

Rocks younger than 65 million years old—no more dinosaur fossils

Thin layer of ancient dust

Rocks 65 million years old—fossil footprints and bones of dinosaurs

Rocks 100 million years old

SITES OF SOME NA

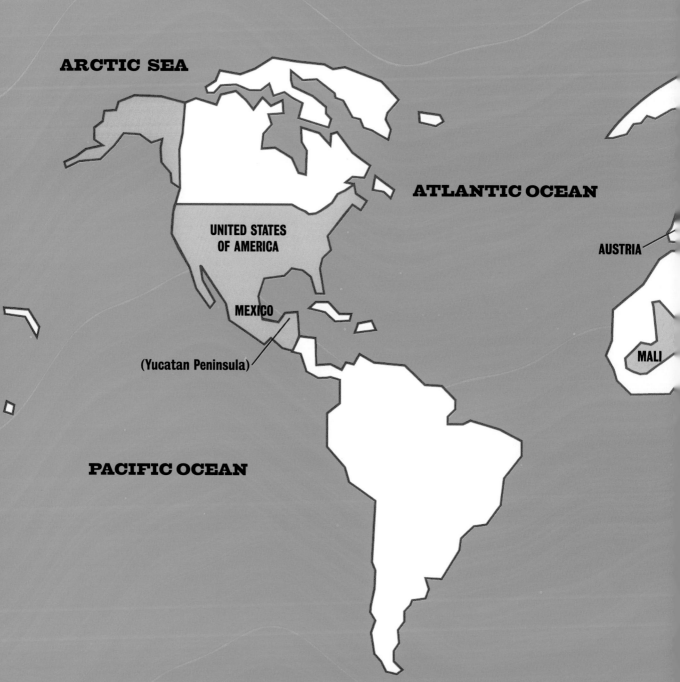

ARCTIC SEA

ATLANTIC OCEAN

UNITED STATES OF AMERICA

AUSTRIA

MEXICO

MALI

(Yucatan Peninsula)

PACIFIC OCEAN

URAL DISASTERS

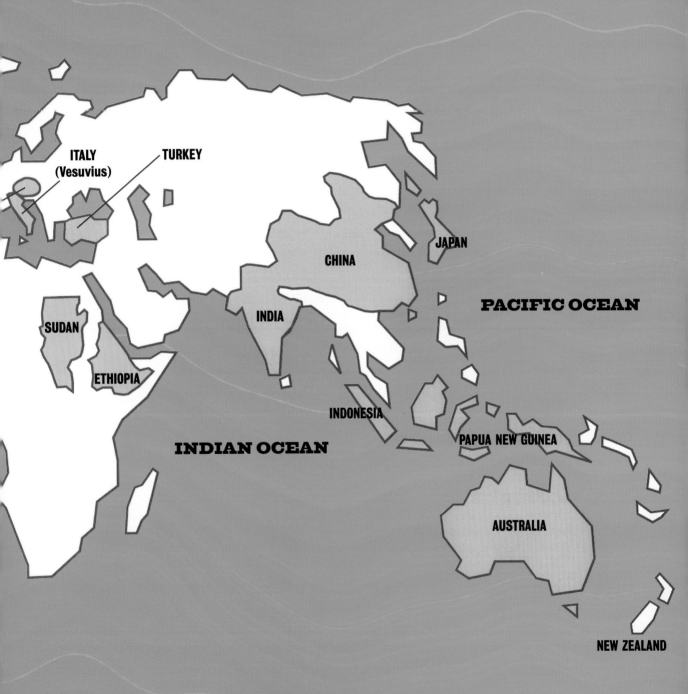

ITALY
(Vesuvius)

TURKEY

SUDAN

ETHIOPIA

CHINA

INDIA

JAPAN

PACIFIC OCEAN

INDONESIA

PAPUA NEW GUINEA

INDIAN OCEAN

AUSTRALIA

NEW ZEALAND

ANTARCTICA

GLOSSARY

active

used to describe a volcano that still erupts

air pressure

the amount of air in a space

atmosphere

the layer of gases around the Earth

Beaufort Scale

a scale used to measure wind speed

crust

the thin, hard outer layer of the Earth

dormant

used to describe a volcano that has not erupted for several hundred years

drought

a long period when there is no rain

earthquake

when the ground shakes

eruption

an explosion of a volcano

extinct

used to describe a very old volcano that will never erupt again; also used to describe animals that are no longer found on Earth

famine

a time when crops do not grow and people have no food

fault line

a crack through layers of rock

flood

river or sea water that flows over the land

fossils

the prints of ancient animals and vegetation in rocks

global warming

the air temperature around the Earth becoming warmer

greenhouse gases

gases that trap the sun's heat in the Earth's atmosphere

hurricane

very strong winds and wet weather

ice pack

ice that floats over the sea

lava

hot molten rock that flows from a volcano

lightning

an electric spark between the ground and clouds

magma

rock from inside the Earth

natural disaster

a natural event that causes problems for people

plates

large slabs of the Earth's crust

sea walls

concrete and stone walls built to protect the coast from the sea

tidal wave

a large wave that comes onshore

tornado

a narrow funnel of fast- spinning air

tsunami

see *tidal wave*

volcano

a mountain that erupts with gases and rock from inside the Earth

INDEX